Software Testing Series

Vol 2 – Test Strategy

Written by:
Michael Pasono

Contents

Overview

About the Author

Michael Pasono is the author behind the *Software Testing Series* who systematically lays out the different areas and concepts of software testing to assure right level of software quality. Technology is continuing to evolve at a rapid pace, this series is meant to familiarize yourself with key software testing concepts.

Michael's professional experience and advocacy in systems quality improvement has him recognized as an industry leader in technology innovations and assuring high quality systems leveraging real-world experiences.

Michael shares key quality topics and recommends approaches to assure a high-quality product is being produced. The recommendations are provided from Michael and not any paid sponsors or previous employers.

Why Important

This Software Testing Series was written to help educate new and advancing software testers that specialize in assuring the quality of a software product or service.

As technology advances rapidly, more software quality control methods are needed to assure proper software quality. These books are meant to introduce you to key topics for you to explore and see how they might fit into your role as a software tester or software quality manager.

The Software Testing Series will be shorter books but focused on a particular topic that might be more relevant to you in your current career. They will range from basic introduction to advanced topics.

We realize time is precious for us in the software testing business trying to keep up with not only new technology but ways to assure quality being produced. This series was meant to be quick reads getting to main topic points and recommendations.

Companies

Large companies are modernizing their technology at a rapid pace to keep up with consumer expectations of an always-on product or service. Companies are taking on new challenges such as digital transformations and cloud migrations.

Not only are these large-scale changes occurring, on-going new threats are appearing more rapidly. These threats are around cybersecurity and data privacy. Board members, shareholders, and CEO's need to address to reduce risk.

With companies collecting so much data as it provides more value, they have to hire quality experts to keep this technology humming and data safe to assure their brand reputation and stay in business. Those of you in the quality assurance and control areas need to stay current or even ahead of these changes coming.

Quality Management Umbrella

Quality management practices have been around for decades. This concept is having a systematic approach to assure processes and control quality testing has transitioned from manufacturing into engineering. This series will cover topics from both Quality Assurance and a Quality Control best practices.

Here is a quick overview of the difference. This is a key area to understand before moving into the series.

Quality Assurance is all about setting up the process in which to conduct quality control. Think of it as umbrella over most testing activities execution. This explanation has helped guide the path to really identifying where in the development life-cycle this quality topic falls into.

Quality Control mainly about the execution of processes defined in Quality Assurance. Testing heavily falls under the control section.

Many companies interchange Quality Assurance with Testing only activity. This is false pretense and this series should debunk that notion of equality.

Software Development

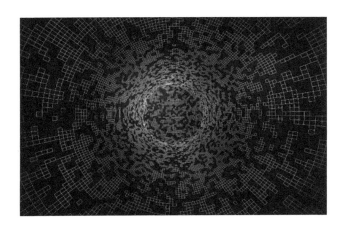

Obviously, software testing has a great deal of interaction with how software should be developed and tested. Software development has rapidly evolved over the years making changes to existing quality control methods and creating new methods.

This series goes over many areas of the software development lifecycle such as requirements to implementation into production and applies key quality assurance and control best practices.

The Software Testing Series

The goal of this series is to introduce new and advanced topics to those interested in learning how to adopt best practices in Quality Assurance and Control.

Key series topics will include the following from those of you beginning your career in software testing to more advanced to help boost your career to that next level:

1) Basics
2) Test Strategy
3) Functional Testing
4) Performance Testing
5) Security Testing
6) Automated Testing
7) Test Data Protection
8) Advanced Methods

Chapter 1 – What is a Test Strategy

Definitions

What is a test strategy and why do I need one? **Test Strategy** is documentation aligned with the test policy that describes the generic requirements for testing and details how to perform testing within an organization.

This documented approach lays out key types of testing needed and how you plan on addressing it. It is the test approach and guidelines you and your company must follow to assure a quality product.

If you are new to software testing many of these key terms are new to you. Within this series we will bold new key terms that are relevant to software testing and provide the definition at that point in time.

Many official testing related definitions are provided by ISTQB and other reputable sources. We will take these standard definitions and expand on key areas throughout this series.

Software is the entire set of programs, procedures, and related documentation associated with a mechanical or electronic system and especially a computer system.

Testing is the process consisting of all lifecycle activities, both static and dynamic, concerned with planning, preparation and evaluation of a component or system and related work products to determine that they satisfy specified requirements, to demonstrate that they are fit for purpose and to detect defects.

Software Testing is defined as an activity within Quality Control to check whether the actual results match the expected results and to ensure that the software system is defect or bug free.

Scope

Identifying the scope of what you need to test is the first critical piece and lays the foundation for defining your test strategy. Think of the scope by identifying what product or service outcome is supposed to be in its ideal-finished state.

In order to properly set this test strategy, identify the business functions that must successfully be executed. Many business functions may span multiple applications or web services in order to accomplish that function.

You need to list all the applications that you need to incorporate into this test strategy. Write them down and continue to reference them and the business functions as you think about detailing out your test strategy.

Clearly setting the scope lets you and your business know to what extent the software testing effort is covering.

If you are in a large organization, you may have one overall test strategy or policy which lays out key approaches for entire QA organization but you also need detailed test strategies for each critical business function.

Chapter 2 – Testing Types

Functional Testing

Once the scope is set, 50-75% of your future tests will be related to functional testing. **Functional Testing** is testing activity performed to evaluate if a component or system satisfies functional requirements.

In short, this is validating WHAT the system does. Think of it as validating business functions from an operational perspective. Typically, these tests are clearly defined as functional requirements (FR) and are used in the development & testing process.

Non-Functional Testing

Testing functionality is a good chuck of your tests but doesn't fulfill a good test strategy. **Non-Functional Testing** is performed to evaluate that a component or system complies with non-functional requirements.

This type of testing focuses on HOW WELL the system works. A large part of this around performance and usability of the system. The additional non-functional testing areas are listed below.

Be sure to fully document how you plan on testing these non-functional activities on a re-occurring basis so they can be repeatable and provide the quality assurance that the system will perform well.

Security Testing

Security testing has really taken center stage lately and is critical to define in your test strategy. If you have experienced any data breaches, you will understand that this section of your test strategy is not to be taken lightly.

Security validation techniques are evolving at a rapid pace but we will cover 3 important areas that are consistent to include in the test strategy.

1) **Penetration Testing** is a testing technique aiming to exploit security vulnerabilities (known or unknown) to gain unauthorized access. This activity should be heavily performed when launching a new product or service prior to GO LIVE.

2) **Static Application Security Testing (SAST)** focuses on white box

security testing. Requires source code and finds vulnerabilities earlier in the software development lifecycle. Fixing these bugs typically cost the least. This activity should be done on each migration of the code base and ideally integrated in an automated fashion.

3) **Dynamic Application Security Testing (DAST)** focuses on black box security testing. Requires application to be running and finds vulnerabilities later in the software development lifecycle. Fixing these bugs typically cost more. This activity should be done on each migration of application.

Usability Testing

The ease of use of the application is critical to define in your test strategy as it can impact sales or revenue. **Usability Testing** is testing to evaluate the degree to which the system can be used by specified users with effectiveness, efficiency and satisfaction in a specified context of use.

The usability of an application can be somewhat objective. It is best to make sure you are focusing on key revenue areas and prioritizing tests based on previous feedback from your end users.

Focus on 2 key questions to answer in your test strategy. How easy is the system to learn and use and how convenient is the system to the end user?

Compatibility Testing

With the expansion of different web browsers and mobile devices, compatibility testing is vital to assure a quality product no matter what viewing method is used. The goal here is to make sure the application can handle these different viewing methods with the least amount of functional or non-functional impacts.

Compatibility testing is the degree to which a website or application can function across different browsers or mobile devices and degrade gracefully when browser features are absent or lacking.

Make sure your test strategy clearly defines out the browsers, operating system, and devices you plan on testing. Include the names, operating systems, and version numbers the application must support.

Performance Testing

When people first think of non-functional testing, they usually think performance first. The reason for this is because many application non-functional issues can be identified within the performance testing umbrella.

Performance testing is testing to determine the performance efficiency of a component or system.

There are many types of performance related tests and the <u>approach to test those types should be clearly defined in your test strategy.</u>

1) **Load** – A type of performance testing conducted to evaluate the behavior of a component or system under varying loads, usually

between anticipated conditions of low, typical, and peak usage.

2) **Volume** – A type of performance testing conducted to evaluate the behavior of a component or system with large volumes of data. Also considered "flood testing". To flood the system with data.

3) **Stress** – A type of performance testing conducted to evaluate a system or component at or beyond the limits of its anticipated or specified workloads, or with reduced availability of resources such as access to memory or servers.

4) **Endurance** – Testing to determine the stability of a system under a significant load over a significant period of time within the system's operational context.

Structural Testing

Structural testing (aka white-box testing) is testing based on an analysis of the internal structure of the component or system. This focuses on how well the code, architecture, and configuration of a component or system is built.

Integration Testing

The purpose of conducting integration tests are to potentially expose defects in the interfaces or in the interactions between integrated components or systems. Integration testing is considered a testing level and not a testing type. A **test level** is linked to the responsibilities of a project.

Definition

A test level that focuses on interactions between systems.

Reasonability

Software Engineer or Software Tester

Importance

Without the proper validation of the integration between components within an application or multiple applications, key data needed to deliver a higher-level business function can fail.

Retest Testing

Once an issue is solidified as a defect or bug, the creator of the software will need to fix. As this gets fixed, you as the software tester will need to re-execute your same test.

This might require you to spend some time resetting test data and re-logging test results. **Re-testing** or **confirmation testing** is simply re-executing same test to help you validate the issue is now gone.

Definition

Re-testing or **Confirmation Testing** - A type of change-related testing performed after fixing a defect to confirm that a failure caused by that defect does not reoccur.

Reasonability

Software Tester

Importance

Re-testing or confirmation testing is important to give closure to an issue that was previously logged by the software tester and corrected by the software engineer. It's a mutual agreement between the creator of the software and the person validating the software features meet the requirement.

Regression Testing

As software application and systems evolve, more and more tests need to be executed to make sure old functionality has not been broken for enhancements. In regards to software testing, these tests are called **regression**. These are test cases that are typically run over and over again expecting the same results to assure no other system issues occurred when introducing new functionality.

These tests validate existing features not impacted by current code changes. These types of tests are a great candidate to automate as they typically require the same test data and same results consistently. Please check out later series on automation to go overall all automation best practices.

Definition

Regression - A type of change-related testing to detect whether defects have been introduced or uncovered in unchanged areas of the software.

Reasonability

Software Tester

Importance

As software features are continuously added and integrated, some level of regression is needed. This validation makes sure no new bugs or defects are a result of new features being added. These tests are against old features that have already been tested in previous releases of the software.

Chapter 3 – Test Management

Test Cases

Now that all the boring prep work is done, the fun begins! Most people that are software testers have a high level of curiosity and passion for breaking things! While it might seem like more fun to spend a majority of your time doing exploratory testing vs prep, prep does go a long way in improving your efficiency to validate and still meet the timeline demands you face.

Definition

Test Case - A set of preconditions, inputs, actions (where applicable), expected results and postconditions, developed based on test conditions.

Reasonability

Software Tester

Importance

Test cases are a critical part of software testing. Test cases hold the logical or process steps (preconditions) you have to take in order to execute the validation (postconditions). Test Cases are typically written in alignment with the requirements of the features in the software.

As you begin executing test cases, this is the moment in time that truly lets you see the quality level of the application. When you execute tests, it's a best practice to log the pass/fail results along with any **bug** or **defects** found. At most companies, they track this effort in a test management tool or system.

Definition

Bug or Defect - An imperfection or deficiency in a work product where it does not meet its requirements or specifications.

Reasonability

Software Engineer

Importance

The logging of a bug or defect is critical to improve the quality of a product or service. This logging notifies the creator or supporter of the software code and allows them the chance to fix the issue. The resolution from the software engineer is required before you can validate the test case.

Traceability

Identifying how you are tracing back your test cases to the requirements need to be included in your test strategy.

Traceability verifies all requirements are tested. One way to link the test cases to the requirements is using a simple matrix. List all the requirements on one axis and list all the test cases on the other axis. Defining how you want to show traceability is what you need in your test strategy.

If you are including your test plan within your test strategy, be sure to spend enough time identifying all the requirements and mapping back to test cases within the matrix.

Requirements and Exit Criteria

Within your test strategy, you must lay out what pre-requisites you have before you can even execute tests. This might be something as simple as getting access to the application and/or getting proper test data setup.

In order to complete the overall testing effort, you must identify what your exit criteria will be to be done. This should be similar to how you have exit criteria for each test case but at a higher level to actually say you are done with testing. This is a critical step to identify as testing efforts can drag on. It should tie back to the scope of the test strategy previously defined.

Defect Management

As your testing strategy gets defined and before you start prepping and execution, you must identify how you are going to track issues logged during execution.

Most large companies will have a separate tool to track test cases and defects in a test management system. Some of the more advanced companies will have this integrated into product backlogs or even code deployment tools. If not, at the very least you will want to leverage excel and some folders to log results and screenshots of any issues found.

You will need to share your results back to the developers to address any issues found.

The defect management part comes into play when developers indicate if issue is a true defect or maybe not. Tracking this is critical so you don't waste time logging issues that were previously found.

Testing Environments

Many companies today have non-production environments that are used to "stage" applications for quality control. The larger the company the more testing environments are typically setup.

In your test strategy, you will want to identify <u>all your testing levels and testing types and indicate which non-production environment the test will be executed in</u>.

Testing Data

Test data is a critical piece to even execute a test. Your test strategy must account for how you plan on getting test data into the test environment and how it needs to be protected. Data protection and data privacy is a critical security approach that needs to be embedded into your test strategy.

For example, if you or your company stores credit card information or personal identifiable information, you must have a process to de-identify or mask sensitive information.

The larger the company the more integrated the test data needs are. Companies typically have a test data management practice which helps developers and testers get the test data they need and in a secured form.

In this series we will have a book just related to data protection. Be sure to check it out if you are accountable or responsible for gathering data for testing.

Standard Tools

Identifying the tools used is critical to maintain order and efficiency if you have a large testing organization.

At a minimum, you need to list all the types of testing that needs to occur and the acceptable tools to leverage. A simple matrix will do.

Communication

Determine how, what, and when to communicate testing progress should be in your test strategy.

Come up with a standard template that shows overall test case and defect metrics. Showing how many test cases have been executed vs the number remaining shows clarity on how much effort is still needed. Also show the defect statues is critical for the development team so they know if they need to research and resolve.

Try to leverage as much automation as possible as some of these metrics to be communicated can be loaded into dashboards or other tools.

Chapter 4 – Testing Responsibilities

RACI

A clearly defined test strategy and how does what is important. For larger QA organizations, the test strategy should indicate who is responsible, accountable, consulted, or informed for each testing activity. A simple matrix can be used.

For example, you might have different quality resources and skillsets for test leads vs test engineers. Typically leads focus on more strategy and planning while engineers focus more on test prep and execution.

You may also have more specialized resources that focus on different areas of testing such as security, performance, data, etc.

Escalation Process

In your test strategy, the escalation process should be clearly defined. There is nothing worse that having a new tester start execution and not knowing who they need to contact for certain situations.

Clearly layout the process flow for defect escalation to be sure everyone knows how defects are being identified, managed, and resolved along with who should be the next point of contact for any resolution.

Metrics and Reporting

The metrics you use in your test
strategy sets the actions for your testers.
Most of us in the QA industry know it is
impossible to test everything given the
recent demands of consumers.

Focus on industry metrics that cover
functional and non-functional testing along
with resolving defects sooner in the
software development lifecycle.

Along with test strategy metrics, is the
communication of these metrics. Define
how you plan on sharing these and what
communication avenues should be clearly
laid out.

Chapter 5 – Test Plan

Test Plan Scope

Once a test strategy is complete, next step is to apply that strategy to a test plan. The test plan is typically time-bound and specific to a new enhancement.

Schedule

The schedule is a start and end date that test prep and execution must occur in.

Process and Data Flows

As new features are developed, process and data flows are likely created. In order to plan and prep for test execution, gather as many process and data flows you can get your hands on. This will help in the test case definition and pass/fail criteria.

Testing Scope and Activity Checklist

Outline each resource, testing level, and testing type in a simple matrix. This will clearly define who is reasonable for what testing activities.   It   might   be   your developers, dedicated testers, or other business partners.

Test Data Planning

If your organization has a set timeline for when test data is available for testing, be sure you are requesting the data you need for the beginning of the test execution window.

Risk Based Planning

Risk based planning is the process of identifying which management, selection, prioritization, and use of testing activities and resources are based on corresponding risk types and risk levels. Risk based planning focuses on spending effort on the highest risk features.

Think of this as targeting testing on the critical features that might impact revenue or sales.

Test Status Reporting

As test execution begins, other people are going to want to know what is the status of testing. This should be a simple and consistent format which outlines the major features: number of test cases and statuses, number of defects and statuses.

Many test management systems can monitor statuses for you but pulling this data and putting it in a simple visual form works best for your stakeholders.

Business Risk Definition

In your test plan, getting valuable information from your key business stakeholders if a feature doesn't work level sets the thoroughness of testing that needs to occur. Remember you likely don't have an infinite amount of time to execute your tests.

Entry and Exit (Acceptance) Criteria

Knowing the pre-requirement for executing a test case known as entry criteria. What do you need in order to execute your tests? This could be as simple as logging the steps to sign-in to a website or mobile device.

The exit (acceptance) criteria are the key items the team agrees upon to say a test case can be "closed". This is typically making sure the test case results are logged in a "passed" status the test management system.

Chapter 6 – Test Strategy vs Test Plan

Comparison

Some QA organizations may leverage a Test Strategy, a Test Plan, or both. The larger the organization and impact to the consumer the likelihood you have both a strategy and a plan.

A test strategy is the over-arching approach to testing at a higher level. It is typically not time-bound and can be repeatable without much change.

A test plan is more specific to a new product or feature being released and is time-bound. The test plan takes the test strategy into account when detailing out.

When to use

It is best practice to split a test strategy and test plan apart. A test strategy typically involves discussions with many different key stakeholders while a test plan can be created mostly by the tester.

A test strategy should be created once and reviewed annually as techniques in testing continue to advance with technology.

A test strategy should be created by a senior level associate which understands QA best practices and knows how the company operates and what drives its revenue.

Maturity

QA testing maturity is something every organization should be striving to improve. The benefits of a mature testing strategy and executing on that strategy limits the potential of damaging quality issues in production.

As within developing a test strategy, each activity within testing has a maturity improvement path. Knowing how to improve each testing activity gets you a step further in limiting damaging quality issues.

Conclusion

Over time… software development and testing best practices evolve, keeping current with new technology and knowing how to test them is always a challenge.

The software testing community is expanding rapidly and becoming more specialized. This requires an open mind to see what is possible and challenge what's possible to assure software testing is keeping up with technology changes.

The mindset of being a software tester is consistent and strong over the decades, technology is not. Learn the basics and then expand. Have a solid background on key software testing concepts and communicating those best practices to key assuring stakeholders.

My hope is this series will help new and current software testers navigate the world of software testing. Not only advancing your knowledge in software testing, but also enable options into broader software quality management best practices or educate others.

The opportunity to enhance yourself are endless. You can focus on broad quality management which covers assurance and control or specialize into a particular area within quality control (i.e. software testing). Only you can determine which path you would like to go!

If you enjoyed this volume on software testing, please stay connected as we release future books on software testing.

Further Reference

The creation of this series is in partnership with Apply QA, LLC; a leading provider of best practices and consultation services for software quality assurance best practices.

Please visit https://applyqa.com to check out their information.

Other References

ISTQB Glossary https://glossary.istqb.org/en/search/

Merriam-Webster https://www.merriam-webster.com/dictionary/software